THE MISGUIDED MENTOR

UNDERSTAND EVERY ASPECT OF MENTORSHIP

BENJAMIN JOHN

Copyright © 2022 by Benjamin John

No portion of this book may be reproduced or transmitted in any form or by any means- electronic, mechanical, photocopy, recording, or otherwise without the prior written permission of the copyright owner.

Paperback ISBN: 979-8-9870951-0-2

Foreword

We all have been misguided at some point in life. But I can confidently tell you what you are about to read; you will not be misguided. What I love about what I do for a living in brand & marketing; I get to hear and share stories that inspire me daily. Whatever you go through in life, there is a song, book, or movie you can relate to. While the *power* of stories is underestimated, what you will see in The Misguided Mentor are stories told so well that they lead to a life-changing, ultimate session.

When I first saw Ben, he had a sign of himself being displayed. The look of determination was written all over his face; as he was preparing to speak, the speech was not what I remembered; it was after.

I saw him genuinely caring and sharing with someone to come away from the perfect pictures they were hiding their personality from. He was a mentor. I could see how much he genuinely cared without expecting anything in return. It's a secret to life when you master it. Ben, the well-put-together, successful business owner, suit-wearing, and well-spoken guy; you would never guess he had overcome so much in life to be in this moment.

Think of a time in life you were misguided. What would've helped you the most? Life tends to be a series of events happening to us, with the people around us, until we *wake up* and realize everyone is put in life for us. This book you are reading right now is happening for you. There is something in this story that will inspire you wherever you are on your journey. Maybe you're a bit misguided now. You don't know where to go. You just want to make sure you are doing all you can so you, too, can be a mentor one day.

The stories in The Misguided Mentor are told in such a way that you may be shocked by what you read. However, Ben has a passion for giving back, reaching back, and helping someone who may be misguided, just like he was.

There is no doubt in my mind that Ben will leave a massive impact on you after reading this book, meeting him, or working with him. The more he tells these stories, the more he will be in demand, as I had witnessed when I told stories of my journey. You will be delighted and encouraged, but most of all, inspired after reading The Misguided Mentor.

Inspire Others Always,

Jeff J. Cunningham

@JeffTheEntrepreneur

Founder Changing Lives Consulting

TABLE OF CONTENT

Prologue	*1*
Making an impact	*3*
My brief story	*6*
Making a difference in people's lives	*51*
Having the right information	*54*
Stages that people need mentorship the most	*56*
Be that mentor in your family	*60*
How a mentor and mentee will benefit you	*62*
Finding your purpose	*64*
How to find the right mentor for you	*67*
The power of a great message	*69*
The power of people	*70*
Unconscious mentoring	*72*
Misguided education	*73*
Be the coach	*75*
Importance of accountability in mentorship	*76*
Getting in the right rooms	*78*
Mentorship during discouragement	*80*
Epilogue	*82*

PROLOGUE

This book is about mentorship's value, different perspectives, and how it has played a significant role in my life. In the first portion of this book, I talk about my journey of mentorship and the experiences I went through in my life. In the second portion, I'll explain how mentorship can and has influenced your life negatively and positively, whether you realize it or not. Next, I'll point out where and when great mentorship is needed most in our lives, families, spouses, and work environments.

I'll be talking about the relationship between a mentor and a mentee. I'll go over different aspects of mentoring, such as finding a mentor, the power of a great message, unconscious mentoring, being the coach, the importance of accountability within a mentorship setting, getting in the right rooms, and much more. This is the perfect book for mentors and mentees. It will enlighten you about the different viewpoints of mentorship and clarify when to be aware of the times mentorship is taking place.

Voluntary and involuntary mentorship is essential to take note of, and in this book, I highlight several areas when this has and is happening in your life, as well as others. This book is for you if you have not actively sought a mentor. If you are considering getting a mentor, this book is for you. If you like a great story about one's adversity and how one came out on the other side victorious, this book is for you. Finally, this book is insightful and thought-provoking if you want to learn how you've been directly or indirectly mentored. If you have been or are thinking about mentoring, you will get massive value from this read.

MAKING AN IMPACT

There is so much power in making a difference in someone's life. Whether a family member, a friend, a coworker, a child, or an adult, there is tremendous value for everyone when an impact is made. This is necessary for us as human beings. We have a natural desire to want to help people. It can be informational, financial, or being available for someone as a mentor or a friend. Sharing is critical for us to connect and grow together.

Information, guidance, and money flow to serve a purpose in one's life. Unfortunately, many people may be misguided and are looking for someone who speaks to them in a way that is unique to them and their experiences in life. When you impact someone's life, they will remember you forever and share the experience. This can be said for both negative and positive experiences.

Naturally, people want a positive experience when they interact with others. But unfortunately, an abundance of negativity in the world is projected and amplified. The news, the radio, coworkers, complainers, family members, spouses, etc. All these sources are designed to focus on the negative, and when it comes to people, they learn this behavior from others and may not even realize that they have that attitude.

The good thing is that this means there is a huge need for people to influence others positively. This can be done in many ways church communities, work environment, mentoring, coaching, and counseling. The possibilities to touch someone and be a positive guide are vast. The world and its people need more resources like this every day.

I would argue that most people can be mentors and have a purpose to help others. However, most people think that mentoring or being a person who shares positive knowledge is not what they are meant for. I disagree. If you think about it, there has undoubtedly been one instance in your life, or many, where someone has looked up to you or turned to you for advice. Young or older individuals, this is proof that people are seeking new information to help them in many ways.

The old saying, "knowledge is power," applies in many ways to coaching and mentoring. For some, it perhaps may be a nice title. But for others, this means something more. When a person has an authentic, genuine, and honest want to help people, that tells me they have a purpose of fulfilling. If you're like me and many others, you enjoy seeing people succeed and, even better, helping guide them to a successful path.

MY BRIEF STORY

At this time in my life, I have been blessed and fortunate to be a mentor for many people. If you had told me seven years ago that I would own two successful businesses, frequently participating in public speaking, being sought after for guidance, writing a book, and creating my own interactive virtual training program, I would've thought you were out of your mind. I am grateful for these opportunities. But it wasn't always this way. I was like many others and was surrounded by negative influences as a child. I grew up in eastern Washington state in a rough environment where I had a survival mentality that I lived by. We lived in a city with one of the highest violent crime rates in the nation. It wasn't easy for our family. I am one of five children my mom had, and I can see that it was hard for her to pay attention to all of us, especially as a single mother. My biological father ultimately left our life when I was very young. Too young to remember. Before he left, he damaged and destroyed us all. Physically and mentally. I have vague memories of him abusing my mom, sister, brother, and me.

Financial stress played a huge factor in my quality of life as well. We didn't have much money, and I remember always living on the bare minimum. This contributed to the hostile atmosphere I lived in. That, combined with the poor school system and community I went to, made it hard for me to find positive influences. But perhaps I wasn't looking hard enough for a mentor to latch on to.

As children, we decide whom we want to be our role models. I, unfortunately, looked for guidance and acceptance from misguided others. Direction can be positive or negative, and you must decide.

Since I chose to look up to people who were making bad choices, this led to me making bad decisions myself. Especially to be accepted and prove myself to the role models I admired. I heard many people tell me, "be careful who you choose as friends." What I didn't understand at the time was that my friends were also my mentors, in a way. Mentors can be bad for you or good for you, depending on who you choose to listen to. People are always looking for someone to value and guide them to their next level of achievement. We do this our whole lives.

Mentors can lead you down the wrong path or show you the correct one. They can let you down or build you up. So be careful who you follow and ensure they have positive and good intentions. More importantly, their will to uplift you and help you reach new levels in life. We should always strive to hit that next level in our lives. Successful people understand that they can always do more and constantly do things to progress and be better each day.

I chose the wrong people to look up to as a child, and my pursuit of acknowledgment from these role models became a part of my life. My actions to prove myself cost heartache to my family and me. I victimized by stealing, lying, and burglarizing. I was unpredictable. I spent much time in juvenile hall for committing crimes. I spent a year in a foster home because my mother couldn't handle my chaotic and destructive behaviors. I wouldn't do well in school because I was too busy trying to impress the wrong people.

Getting older, I began to change my behavior. I looked for other sources to guide me and become a more positive, safe haven for me. My stepfather, brother-in-law, and a few others were individuals I started to look up to because I could see they had good values and morals. They worked hard, cared for their families, and positively influenced my life. One of the main things I learned is that they were loyal to the companies they worked for. I was taught to find a good job, save money, buy a home, start a family, be happy with what I got, retire, and live happily ever after. This was a mindset I later had to rewire to achieve the success I wanted for myself entirely and that I was meant for.

I wish I could say that I got it together after looking up to my stepfather, brother-in-law, and other great role models, but unfortunately, I was still misguided and unfulfilled in a different way. It wasn't until almost twenty years later that I realized my life was meant for more. Even though they had good intentions, it seemed like their advice didn't fit what I wanted to do. Even though I didn't know what I wanted to be, I knew I had a bigger purpose.

At the age of 19, I found myself working at a retail store for two years. During this period, I was misguided and confused about what I wanted to do with my life. I had no directions and no long-term plan. I fell into a life of drug use and became completely influenced to live this terrible lifestyle. Smoking weed all day for about twenty years and smoking crack at age 19 for two years was my new life of bad habits. Sounds bad? That's because it was. It was one of the worst times in my life. Not only was I disappointed in my actions. I was upset that I had been making decisions that wouldn't improve my life position. When I think about it now, guidance and mentorship is what I was craving, and a lack of the proper guidance contributed to the place that I was in. Yes, these were my own bad decisions, but more importantly, a lot of that could've been avoided if I had taken accountability and actively sought out the proper role model for my life. Finally, I accepted that I was killing myself and going nowhere in life.

I realized that to find my purpose, I needed to be honest with myself and give up my old way of thinking to do something different. Something that no one in my family has ever done. Eleven years later, I developed a desire and a calling not to be average but extraordinary. To not lay low but to help people and contribute to others in their pursuit of greatness. Not be satisfied but be hungry for more knowledge and achievements and not retire with the bare minimum income, but to have an abundance of it and set my family up with a path to financial freedom as mine and their legacy.

This didn't become a passion of mine until my early thirties. I went through life getting the experience of working different jobs. I got my first couple of jobs while in high school. My first job was working for the fast-food industry at age sixteen. I then transitioned into working at a meat packing company after that. I worked as a telemarketer for almost a year as well. I enjoyed it because it was my first sales position, and I learned I was good at it. I also worked numerous retail jobs. But the most pivotal job I had was the last one I ever worked because that was when I transitioned into being a leader and a boss immediately after this experience.

From twenty-two to thirty-two, I worked as a lead carpenter building high-end outdoor living improvements such as sunrooms, screen rooms, decks, patio covers, handrails, awnings, and power screens. Although this was not a job I wanted to spend the rest of my life working at, I learned many things about myself and people during these ten years. I knew that I could do anything, physically and mentally, that I put my mind to. I learned how to work with people, how to communicate, and how to treat people right. I learned that there are many types of characteristics and personalities within an individual.

I had good experiences and learned a lot during this time, but some of the main things I learned from working that long for one company was that *no one will ever be able to pay you what you're worth*. So you either work hard on your dreams, or you work hard building someone else's. I learned that I was not fulfilled, and I had this nagging feeling that I was meant for something more and that I was not living my full potential.

I would work all day, be burnt out, smoke weed, check out of life, and not work on anything else for myself. I became complacent and comfortable. I thought that working for one company for thirty years, saving money for retirement, and not asking questions was how I was supposed to live my life.

That is because I was subconsciously taught by observing my immediate circle of friends, family, the school system, and coworkers that this was the way to live. Of course, I love my friends and family, but it was my understanding that they were, perhaps, misguided. Not in a direct way but in a way that they thought and were taught was the correct way to live.

You see, what may be suitable for someone else, may not be right for you. Chances are, if you dig deep within your thoughts, you will likely feel that something is missing in your life. If so, I encourage people to lean on that and explore why that is a little more. Like I said before, I believe that everyone has something more that they can do and, more importantly, a lot more that they can offer to themselves and others.

In my case, I couldn't shake the thought of me being a carpenter until I retired. I couldn't accept not offering something more to myself, my daughter, my future, or others. Whenever I helped someone else solve a problem, I would get so much pleasure. It only made sense to put myself in a position to help others as much as possible.

Around the ten-year mark of working for this company, I was approached and propositioned by a friend to quit my job and start a business with her. It was perfect timing since I thought of doing bigger things in life. We met about eight years prior when I built a sunroom for her while working for this company. I continued to do steady side work for her because she loved my work ethic and efficiency. I would do odd jobs for her around the house. She never stopped improving her home in some fashion, so she kept me busy when I needed to make extra money.

She was an intelligent and ambitious woman. I considered her to be a successful person. She owned apartment buildings, worked for a top-tier airline manufacturing company, and always looked for that next thing. She was a multi-millionaire that was money driven. When I saw her motivation to chase money, I thought that was the way to be when you want to achieve success. For months, we would go to different business seminars together, exploring various options on what business we wanted to get involved in. We would ask each other, "is this something we could get rich doing?"

We thought about flipping homes, buying a fast-food franchise, building storage units, and other possibilities. At the time, the 502-Marijuana industry had just become legal and increasingly popular in the Pacific Northwest. Many people who got involved early made a lot of money growing and distributing this product. Ultimately, this was the industry that caught my business partner's eye because of the cash flow that was possible to achieve. Me and her knew nothing about it. The only thing I knew was how to smoke it. I didn't know the first thing about growing and selling marijuana. We both decided it was something we wanted to get involved with because of the profit potential.

We would grow, sell, and become millionaires, we thought. When we started seriously thinking about doing this and committed to start putting things in place to start this business venture, it was brought to my attention by her that I couldn't continue to work my job and that I would have to go all-in on this project.

"You know you will have to quit your job to do this?" she said.

The thought had never even crossed my mind when she said that, and it scared me. I thought I could try and do this; if it failed, I could fall back on what I was comfortable doing. I had a hard time accepting that I would have to take a considerable risk and walk away from a job I had for ten years. I was comfortable, average, and complacent. I didn't take enormous risks. I didn't put myself in a position that could leave me with nothing if I failed. This was going to be a whole new experience for me.

After thinking about it for a couple of weeks, I decided to do it. I didn't know if I would be successful. I didn't know if I was making the right choice. What I did know was that I was not happy with the trajectory of my life, my finances, and that feeling of being capable of doing more with myself and not taking action. I knew I needed to take this step in my life, whether it was a success or a failure. I knew I needed this change.

At the same time, a part of me was excited because of the sense of uncertainty that came with this decision. I had never made a change of this magnitude or in the entire ten years of working as a carpenter. Safe can be both good and dangerous. It's good because you never put yourself in harm's way and never take chances. It's dangerous because you never take chances, get uncomfortable, and never mentally grow. I understood I was putting myself in a situation where I was mentally improving. The combination of that and the new money I could be making attracted me to this plan of ours.

We first began by locating a property to build this business and grow the product. We found this old house with an old R.V. storage directly behind it. It hadn't been in operation for years, and the owner was simply renting it out to an individual living in it and not maintaining the R.V. storage area in the backyard. As a result, the house was outdated, run-down, and needed to be cleaned up to be suitable to live in.

Although the current renter was living in it (preparing to move out), it was a filthy and uninhabitable place. Behind the house was a huge storage space that looked like it hadn't been used in over twenty years. The storage space was two hundred feet long, twenty feet from front to back, and fourteen feet in height. Every storage space was divided into twenty-foot sections. This made it ten, twenty by twenty areas per space. It was made of old steel posts that had steel panels along the back of it and the two sides of it. It had one old R.V. sitting in one of the spaces, and it looked like it had been abandoned for some time. So we had our work cut out for us.

The landlord we purchased the property from gave the current tenant an eviction notice. Once the tenants moved out, we began the property improvements; that would be where my three-year-old daughter and I would live. We wanted to ensure the place was fixed and more livable. After replacing the toilet, painting the house, and landscaping, we began taking this old building and turning it into a fully functional operation that would yield us enough product to sell and make the amount of money we predicted. This was an intimidating task because we knew nothing about the weed-growing business.

Although I was very confident and good at looking up "how to" videos online to help me with things I had never done before, this was a big project. I started by installing over five hundred feet of barbed wire fence with privacy fabric around the entire property. After that, I rented a backhoe to begin digging for the electrical, gas, and cable lines needed to run this new building.

The power would be used for the grow lights, air conditioners, co2 burners, and all necessary powered appliances for the growing process. I had never used a backhoe. I had never connected gas lines, and I most certainly never connected an HVAC system. It was all completely new to me. There was a sense of urgency to get this plan up and running because of the amount of startup money my partner was hemorrhaging to fund this project. It cost about a half million dollars. So, there was much pressure to produce.

After nine months of hiring and firing people, we finally finished it. The building was complete, and we were ready to start growing. We hired a professional grower to help us begin the process. This was supposed to be a great arrangement because he claimed he knew someone who would want to buy everything we had when it was ready. Unfortunately, he was not the promptest or business-oriented individual to work with, and we struggled to get him to commit to timelines. We eventually fired him. He was able to work with me long enough to where I got the basics of how to operate this business by myself, but it took several months and a few failures to get this process down. I didn't know how much work it would take to do this. I had a four thousand square foot building that had thirty-six, thousand-watt lights that were split up into a perpetual system. We set it up with water hookups and one-hundred-gallon reservoirs for feeding the plants. We had a large hanging and drying area to cure everything and prepare it for sale. It was a very long process that I was unprepared for. However, I soon acclimated myself to the procedure. It involved recruiting some of my local friends for some of the more uncomplicated harvesting help I needed. It was a lot of late nights of us in the grow shop, just listening to music, trimming, watering, and harvesting plants. After walking away from my job of ten years, I was invested in making this successful.

After getting to the point where we had produced some finished product to sell in the black market (the black market was a term meaning that we were doing it illegally), the time came to figure out how to find people to sell to. This was going to be a challenge. The only thing I thought of was asking people and advertising online. For obvious reasons, using an online platform to find leads was the most dangerous. The main one was that I didn't know the people and was dealing with thousands of dollars in transactions. Slowly, I was able to sell to people and make some money. I would give every penny to my business partner until we got significantly closer to reimbursing the startup cost. Even though I had about one hundred thousand dollars of sweat equity into the buildings and didn't sign a contract with her in this business venture, I trusted her.

I started out being pretty successful for months. But it became increasingly harder. The online platform started to delete my posts, my sales experience was poor, and the competition was high. We were not the best on the market either. This led me to take more risks. I would meet people from out of state who would fly into town, purchase the product, and then ship it in the mail to the designated destination. I found myself in very dangerous, highly stressful, and nerve-racking situations. There were several occasions where I would be in a room with multiple people I didn't know, counting anywhere from thirty to fifty thousand dollars in fives, tens, and twenty-dollar bills. This was a situation that I never got used to because it took time. I had to look over my shoulder while counting large stacks of money, and I never knew if one of them intended to rob me.

The most life-changing experience I had during this was when I got robbed. Like any other prospect call, I talked to this local individual, and he said he wanted a few pounds. Back then, a few pounds could start at four hundred dollars and work its way to five thousand dollars. He tells me what city he is in, and I establish a place to meet and do the transaction. I told him to meet me at his neighborhood gas station. I usually meet people in a public area before doing business with anyone. So, I thought this would be an excellent place to meet. As I pulled into the gas station, I called him and told him I was waiting for him. As I saw him walk up to the truck, I noticed that he was with two other individuals. That immediately seemed suspicious to me. I told him to get in the truck by himself and that his friends would have to wait by the store. He said, "ok." He hops in the truck and begins to look at the product closely. He started to smell and squeeze it.

"Hmm, this is pretty good. Also, can my brother look at it since he's paying for half?" he asked.

He points to his brother, who is waiting by the store with an innocent look on his face.

I said, "sure."

His brother and the other individual started to walk over to my truck. Now I have all three looking at the products. One is in the front seat, and the other two are standing by, waiting for each other to decide. I didn't know that the decision they would make would change me forever. As they were observing the weed, in a blink of an eye, they grabbed the few pounds in reach and started running down the road. Out of instinct, I immediately began to go after them in my truck. I didn't know what I was going to do. It was just my first instinct. I was so emotionally and financially invested in the product that I didn't know what to do.

As I drove the truck out of the parking lot, tires squealing and aimed toward the direction they had run; I saw them all running on the sidewalk. I rolled my window down when I got closer and began to yell, "stop." Two of the guys ran in different directions between some houses, but one of the individuals stopped right in his tracks, turned around, pointed a gun at me, and fired two shots. All I saw were two flashes, and I heard two loud pops. Without thinking, my fight-or-flight instincts kicked in. I put the truck in reverse and quickly drove out of there. I parked up the street to process what happened. I didn't think I was shot but couldn't believe it. But, of course, I didn't believe it.

I called my next appointment to let him know what had happened. He was someone I'd already dealt with before and established some trust.

"I just got robbed and shot at," I told him.

"Really? Were you hit?" he asked.

He was genuinely concerned. As I heard the cop's sirens coming from different directions, I stopped to think and closely started to examine my body. I patted around my chest to ensure I wasn't hit. You see, I knew from watching movies or documentaries that there could be a good chance that I was shot, but I didn't realize it because of the shock and adrenaline I was experiencing. After checking my body, I responded,

"No, I wasn't hit."

I then took a peek outside my window towards the door area and noticed two bullet holes in the side of my truck about two inches below the windowsill, where you would rest your arm with the window down. This rushing sensation instantly came over me in a second. I realized how close to dying I just came. I couldn't believe it. Still, on the phone, I said,

"They hit my truck and almost killed me."

"No way?" he said.

I proceeded with my two other appointments that night. I just wanted to get home as soon as possible and think about what had just happened. It was one of the most terrifying things that I had experienced in my life. You would think that after something like that, I would stop and, more specifically, not even finish the remaining appointments for the night. But I didn't. I was too focused on chasing money. This was something that I thought I needed to do to be successful by observing my business partner. I looked up to her a great deal. Yet, I realized that we were both misguided in thinking that money was the answer to everything and at all costs. I finished the night safely and made two successful sales after that intense encounter. I went home that night and had a tough time sleeping because of the thoughts that went through my head.

"Would if I had died?"

"Who would take care of my daughter?"

"What would happen to her life if I was gone?"

Questions I asked myself. It got me thinking about my actions and how to do things differently now.

The following day I looked at the two bullet holes in my truck. I guess I was hoping that it was all just a bad dream. I was wrong. They were there and right in front of me. I drove that same truck for over a year, and every time I got into it, I had to look at the holes as a reminder. They were haunting me. I looked closely at the truck to see where the bullets had hit and why they didn't go through the truck door and hit me in the chest. I started to shine a light through the dark holes to understand better what had happened. I then saw this small metal bar that was very thin inside the door.

As I look even closer, I can see exactly where the two bullets directly hit this bar, ricochet, and were deflected to stay in the door.

It was a complete miracle that it did not go through the door and hit me right in the chest. Once again, I was shocked and in disbelief.

The next day I called my business partner to show and tell her what had happened. She took a look at the door.

"Those aren't bullet holes," she says.

I immediately got offended. I wasn't sure what she was accusing or doubting me of. It caught me off-guard.

"Of course they are! Look at it! Do you think I'm lying and put holes in my truck?" I asked.

"Maybe," she stated.

This was when I realized our relationship was not built on trust, which changed the dynamic. I was out here risking my life, and she had no appreciation for it nor a concept of the level of risk I was out here taking every day. I felt highly disrespected and looked at her very differently after that moment.

It got worse from there. I noticed a growing disrespect from her as time went on. One day I met with her at her house, and I brought my daughter. I knew she didn't like children much. But I didn't realize how extreme she was when it came to that. I soon found out. As we showed up at her house to meet her, I called her and told her I was outside waiting.

"Come in," she said.

We walked into her office.

"You brought *it* with you?" she asked.

I snapped back and said,

"Hey," be more respectful to my daughter. She's just a little girl. They are impressionable, and hearing things like that is very hurtful. Especially at a young age."

She sat there and stared at me without a response. She looked confused, as if I was speaking a different language.

A few days passed after the shooting, and I had this curious feeling come over me to check the news and see if there had been any more shootings in that neighborhood. So I started scrolling through the online news feeds. To my surprise, I saw this article, "Man found shot and dead in his car. A possible drug deal gone bad. Three suspects in custody." I couldn't believe it. I envisioned this poor dead man being me and realized that this could have easily been the outcome for me on the same night I encountered those three men. It gave me chills and made me realize how fortunate I was to still be alive.

As I was regrouping from the recent near-death experience, I was trying to think of a better way not to go into the dangerous streets and sell products to people I didn't know too well. I started to brainstorm ways to reduce or eliminate the number of times I'd have to meet people I didn't know. I was beginning to worry and didn't want to be robbed again. I didn't want to put my life in danger. I quickly understood that this was a life-risking industry and that going places to meet people was not the best approach.

When I was trying to think of a way to try something different, one of my current customers asked me if I would be comfortable shipping the product out of state to him. This was an individual who would fly over and usually ship it himself. When he asked me, I was immediately not interested because I was petrified of the possibility of getting caught and going to prison. He then explained how he did it and how he could conceal the odor in the shipping process. After hearing him speak about it, I decided that I would be willing to give it a try and take the risk. First, he would send me twenty thousand dollars. Then, I'd send him ten pounds of weed in the mail.

"What could be so hard about that?" I asked myself.

I didn't realize how stressful this whole process would be. On paper, it sounded great. But going through it was a different story. First, we agreed on a deal; then, he gave instructions.

"Go, open a P.O. Box, and I'll send you the money," he said.

So, I went, opened up a P.O. Box for him to send the money, and a few days later, I received a large letter from "Mike." Not sure if that was his real name, but that was who he called himself. I took the letter and drove back to the house. When I got there, I immediately began to open it anxiously. A part of me was curious to see if he did send the money, and another part of me was hoping that he didn't so that I wouldn't have to go through with it. As I opened the letter, I saw that it was a magazine. I began turning the pages, and what did I see? One-hundred-dollar bills taped to the inside of each page. I carefully removed the tape and started to count the money. It added up to twenty thousand dollars. Just like he said. I was shocked. But now, I thought, I will have to go through with this.

I'll never forget the first time I took ten pounds of cannabis into the post office to send in the mail. As I pulled into the post office parking lot, I started to convince myself that I shouldn't do it and send him back his money. The pressure and anxiety increased. I sat in my truck for an extended time, trying to nudge myself just to do it. Finally, I got out of the truck and proceeded to the post office entrance. As I walked in, I immediately noticed a massive line of people. That instantly added to the pressure I was feeling. As I stood in the long line that seemed like it was not moving, I started to think that I smelled weed either on me or coming out of the box. This started to get me worried.

"Did I package it well enough? Do I have the smell on me? Will they smell it and pull me aside or call the cops?" I said to myself. When I reached the front counter, I placed the box on the weight scale.

"Are there any perishable items or liquids?" the cashier asked.

"No," I quickly answered.

Then he asked, "standard shipping or express?"

"Standard," I replied.

"Great," he said and handed me a receipt.

I headed out the door and felt relief when that experience was over. I walked back to my truck, hoping that nothing would go wrong or the package wouldn't get intercepted. For the next three days, I was worried about it making it over safely. Then, on the third day, I got a call from Mike.

"I got the package, and everything looks good," he said.

That was what I was waiting to hear. He followed up with,

"I'm going to send you the same amount. Let's do it again."

"Yes, of course," I responded.

That was the beginning of me taking a different kind of risk for the following year. I ended up shipping out approximately two hundred pounds of weed to several locations and individuals before I ended up leaving the industry.

My business partner and I never hit the projected numbers we anticipated, and tension increased between us. We were not on track to becoming the millionaires we thought we would be, and things started to look doubtful. I was doing much better than I was as a carpenter, but it wasn't bringing the income that either of us expected, and as time passed, the industry drastically changed. The market flooded, and prices went substantially lower, making things harder. In addition, at that time, marijuana became legal in our region and was more available to the public. So, there was no need for the local leads to keep doing business with us. It was primarily isolated to out-of-state shipments for us.

During this time, I realized that I hadn't made much money and was giving it all directly to my business partner until we paid this debt back. I brought in about a quarter million dollars in eighteen months. These are not the best numbers, but it was a huge accomplishment for someone like me to convert from carpenter to sales rep to grower. I was happy I was doing something different and could bring in that revenue with pure hustle. Even though I managed to bring in some money, it wasn't coming in fast enough, and I wasn't enjoying putting my life and freedom on the line every day. It became so overwhelming, and I found myself asking the same question. "Is this what I was meant for? Am I living my full potential?"

Of course, I knew in my heart that I was meant to do something more. I still didn't know what it was, though. The relationship between my business partner and I was toxic and mentally taxing. After two years of working with her, I decided to separate and try and figure out what I would do next. So, my daughter and I moved out. Unfortunately, I thought the cannabis industry was still the answer to my financial freedom. So, I decided to reach out to a good friend and move into his house. He was married to my sister about twenty-five years prior, and I still maintained contact with him as a good friend. He was able to clear out a room and make space for me to get on my feet as I started over.

I proposed that I wanted to convert his rental house into a "grow operation." Since I knew I could bring in money that way, I also started sub-contracting work for an individual I was introduced to in the general contracting business. I would build several styles of sunrooms, decks, and patio cover jobs. Between those two incomes, I was able to get some money set aside. My brother-in-law lived out in the country, and it was hard for me to commute that far. So, I knew I didn't want to stay out there for a long time.

During the time that I had spent with my business partner and the time I lived with my brother-in-law, my daughter's grandparents helped watch her while I raised money. Unfortunately, I had to make the tough decision and let her be with her grandparents during this transition. I didn't want her to be exposed to that environment or danger. It was tough because I didn't want her to feel abandoned. Mainly because her mother was not involved in our lives for a few years, leaving me to be a single dad for a long time. I missed spending quality time with my daughter.

When I was living with my brother-in-law, my daughter was about five years old and growing fast. I felt a sense of urgency to get into my own place and put us in a situation where we could spend more time together. I found myself, yet again, working long hours into the night. Sometimes, I would work until 2 in the morning and wake up at 6 AM to work construction jobs during the day. This arrangement demanded a lot of effort and perseverance. It required a lot of physical and mental energy and was extremely hard. I was constantly depleted and tired most of the day. One late night, I felt how much I was being drained and almost paid for it with my life.

Along with my jobs, I had committed to playing in a band and devoted much effort to that project. Primordial Atrocity, we called ourselves. It was a band formed after I heavily searched for musicians to collaborate with. Finally, I found a good group of guys to play with and enjoyed it. It was my outlet, escape, and passion. I never thought I would be a musician in my life. When I was twenty-five years old, I picked up the guitar and instantly became hooked on the writing and creating process. It was challenging, and it felt so rewarding to complete a track to present to people. The reaction when they heard it was a great feeling and became addicting. This fed my passion to pursue the musical journey. We quickly became known in our local community as a serious band that wanted to be known.

On this particular night, we had a show in Seattle that went late into the night. The previous night, I spent several hours taking care of the plants in the operation at my brother-in-law's house—one of those nights that required me to stay up until 3 in the morning. Then, I went to sleep and woke up at about 6 AM the same morning. It was a hectic day. First, I went to work on a construction site to make some money. After that, I immediately prepared for the show in Seattle. I was still selling large amounts of product at this time and would have a few pounds on me, just in case. Also, since I had my contacts in different states and was waiting for my crop to harvest, I could supplement my income by selling another grower's product during the wait time.

We went to Seattle and had a fantastic show. We played with a couple of other bands, one that included an overseas band feature. After our show, I had to drive back to my brother-in-law's, which was over a two-hour drive. I didn't think much of it until I hit the road and realized I was exhausted and running on three hours of sleep from the night before. I made it about halfway home and noticed I was slightly dozing off while driving and catching myself falling asleep briefly. I tried different things to keep awake, such as rolling the window down and listening to loud music. It helped, but it wasn't waking me up. Finally, as I got to the last five miles of my long ride, I had this strong feeling of pulling over and going to sleep for a bit. I thought this would be silly because I was about ten to fifteen minutes from my destination.

"I made it this far, and I'm only a few miles from my house," I told myself.

I never had a moment where I felt I needed to pull over. I should've listened to my instincts. This would be a near-death experience that I would never forget.

As I proceeded to take a chance and push forward to my brother-in-law's house, I started thinking to myself, "I can do this." My eyes began to close slowly. I occasionally woke up, then went into a deep daze. I began to hear and feel a vibration. It was as if I was on a train that had derailed. I opened my eyes and instantly realized I was off the road. I was on the opposite side of the two-lane road where oncoming traffic would typically be approaching. My instinct was to jerk the wheel to the right to stay on the road. Unfortunately, in a panic, I cranked the steering wheel a bit too much and over-corrected. I shot back onto the road so hard that the truck did a 180-degree turn and went back across the entire road once more, crashing into a ditch, where my body slammed into the driver's side door. I sat there and collected myself in shock. Adrenaline was pumping, and I immediately thought about the cannabis in the toolbox in the back of the truck bed. I knew I had to get the product and hide it before anyone showed up to ask questions about it. I also knew I could go to jail and get criminal charges for having that amount on me.

I got out of the vehicle and noticed the toolbox had disconnected from the back of the truck. Lying upside down in a ditch, I flip the toolbox over. My weed was inside of it. I grabbed the bucket and started heading up the steep ditch in the pitch-black dark, where the porch lights of the few houses in the distance slightly illuminated the area for me to see. Remember, this was deep in the Washington forest and out in the middle of nowhere. At the very moment when I got to the top of the ditch to throw the bucket in the closest bush, I saw a sheriff quickly showing up with his lights flashing.

He got on his intercom and said,

"Hold it; what did you just throw over there?"

I said nothing in response. I stood there, hoping he would pretend he didn't see what I'd done. Unfortunately, I wasn't so lucky. A second sheriff showed up with his lights flashing as well. I began to worry. I started thinking of the worst scenarios and imagined myself getting handcuffed and taken to jail. Thoughts of my daughter started going through my mind. The look of sadness on her face teared me up. The idea of me not being with her scared me the most. I stood there, listening to the two sheriffs talk-

"He threw something in the bushes over there," one said to the other. As the Officer went to look for the bucket I had thrown, my heart began to race. I didn't know what was going to happen. He quickly found it and brought it over.

He placed it on the ground right before me and opened it. Immediately he saw the four pounds that were tightly packed in the bucket. A pungent odor came out of the bucket and hit us both in the face. We smelled it instantly. The Officer pulled each bag out, one by one,

"Is this just marijuana," he asked.

"Yes," I replied.

"Why were you hiding it from us? You know it's legal here, right?"

I hesitated for a second, then said,

"I reacted that way because I worried you would take it."

"If it's not hard drugs, we don't care," he said.

"Oh," that was all I could say.

"Do you have someone you can call to pick you up?" he asked.

"Yes," I responded.

I quickly called my brother-in-law to come pick me up. He was only a couple of miles up the road. It didn't take long for him to show up, and when he did, I quickly headed towards the vehicle to hop in. On the way over, the Sheriff said,

"Don't leave just yet."

I began to tell my brother-in-law what had happened, and he couldn't believe it. The Officer came over to the vehicle and handed me a ticket for speeding. He said,

"I have to charge you for something. I will not charge you for the excess cannabis in your possession, so you should be thankful for that. Drive safe and pick up your truck as soon as possible."

"Yes sir," I responded, and we drove off.

That night I had difficulty sleeping, considering I had just fallen asleep at the wheel.

I was too worried about getting a new truck to continue my carpentry work. But, more importantly, I was having a moment and asked myself,

"why am I risking my safety and life to continue pursuing the cannabis industry?"

It was too dangerous. I realized I wasn't thinking of my daughter, I wasn't thinking of my future, and I wasn't thinking of how I was not getting ahead in life. So, it was time for another change.

The following week I was thinking of what I needed to do to get out of the living situation with my brother-in-law. It was too far from the city and unsuitable for me. I had invested so much time and money into the home operation that I needed to sell the products at hand before I stopped. Then use that money as a down payment into a new place. A month later, I finally harvested the product I needed. Soon after that, I was sitting at the table trying to brainstorm what kind of change I could make to get financially ahead. I wasn't quite sure; I knew that working for others wasn't a position I preferred. It demanded a lot of time and didn't provide me any freedom. I didn't like working for someone else any longer, especially after working for myself with my business partner for two years.

That night I was talking to my nephew, and he said,

"Why don't you start your own business?"

"I don't know, I never thought of it before," I replied.

I realized nothing was stopping me from doing that, except that I had not decided to do it. So that night, I stayed up and hand-drew a logo for the company. The idea immediately came to me, and I couldn't let it go until I got it on paper. Surprisingly, it is the same logo I have used for the company for the last five years. Once that was done, it felt a little more natural. I was going to do this, I thought. I was nervous and excited all at once. I had never run a legal business by myself and knew nothing about what I was getting myself into. I never took a course on business or accounting. Once again, I was going to start something new and put myself in high discomfort.

I have noticed from being uncomfortable that I learn and mentally grow so much from experience. Mainly because I always seem to figure out how to navigate the obstacles and problem-solve the issues that arise during the journey. I knew I had a gift to put in massive amounts of action and effort to accomplish a task.

I learned this about myself when I worked all the jobs before where I am today. I noticed that I always separated myself from the rest of the average workers. This is because I always wanted to be remembered and valued as a hard worker and not considered someone looking to get by. I would say that I got this quality from observing these individuals in my life; my stepfather, brother-in-law, and even my brother. They all worked hard. To me, they stood out because of that. So that fed my desire to stand out even more. Because those were my role models, they were the people I looked up to. Anyone who caught my attention as a hard worker always made an impression in my mind, and I never forgot it.

After ten months, the day finally came when I was going to move out from under my brother-in-law, rent my own place, start my own business, and get to spend more time with my daughter. I was excited and just wanted to hit the ground running to make something of myself. I knew that I was getting closer to reaching my capabilities of success. Of course, I still didn't know what that was exactly. But I knew I was pushing forward and doing things nobody in my life was doing. I observed that no one in my family had ever started a business or gone outside their comfort zone.

I eventually found a place to live in that was closer to the city. It was difficult after destroying my credit when I left my job. I had no proof of income for over two years, especially after the two-year business endeavor with my business partner. She kept every single penny that ever came in from that operation. Thankfully, I could put down about three thousand dollars for the first month and last month's rent to a company that gave me a chance. I quickly moved in and acclimated to the new environment and neighborhood. It was quite the change from the country living I was used to in the prior year at my brother-in-law's house. I lived next door to a local elementary school and across the street from the adjacent high school. It was a lovely area to be in.

The next step was to get my daughter back full-time and registered at the school next door to our house. At first, I didn't get her involved with daycare because I didn't have the money for it. Fortunately, my best friend was able to help me for a few months. He came to live with me and would pick up my daughter from school while I was working. The business was new, and I was still getting used to marketing, networking, scaling the company, and physically working on the job sites. This became overwhelming because I realized that I couldn't do everything, and it was nearly impossible to grow the business while doing everything in it. I worked on it, but not as much as I'd liked.

I began to establish a social media presence on a handful of platforms commonly used by the community. This started to generate leads for my company, and I began to get busier and busier, which is what most businesses wanted. So, I started hiring to help with the workload. I worked during the day, stayed up late, posted content, and boosting social media ads to get more traffic to my sites.

On top of that, I was not making that much money from the business. I was underbidding jobs, making little money, and not getting enough attention for people to know me. I had been underestimating the effort it took to become omnipresent, to be everywhere, all of the time. I knew nothing about this. Until I stumbled upon my mentor; he would change how I looked at business and life and how I would start living my own life from there on.

One day I was hanging out with my nephew, and he handed me a book titled "The 10X Rule," by Grant Cardone.

"You should check this out," my nephew said.

I considered my nephew smart and believed he understood what I valued and was interested in. So, I trusted his judgment. I started to read the book a little bit and then drifted away from it as I got more involved with my business. It sat on my table for a couple of weeks. My nephew asked,

"Have you finished the book?"

"No," I replied.

Then I began to make excuses for why I hadn't kept reading it. I hadn't read a book in several years before that one.

"I'm going to burn the audiobook onto a CD for you to listen to in your truck," my nephew stated.

"Cool," I said back to him.

A week goes by, and he hands me the CD collection. Immediately when I popped the CD into the player and began to listen to this man (Grant Cardone), I had a connection with his voice and a sense of familiarity. I don't know why, but I thoroughly listened to him and his message in the book. It drew me in. I related to him so much. I also understood the bullet points he drove home to the listener. His message was clear, and I began to obsess over what he was saying because I knew it made perfect sense. It painted a clear picture of why I lacked certain things in life. He gave me a clear direction on what I should and shouldn't be doing in my business, parenting, and friendships. Some of the main things that stuck with me were impactful and resonate with me even now.

Some of the main points that stuck out to me were money follows attention and quantity over quality. Omnipresence over obscurity and service is senior to the sale. This was the home runner for me; *things are not happening to you but because of you.* I knew then that Grant Cardone was the perfect mentor for me.

MAKING A DIFFERENCE IN PEOPLE'S LIVES

When I reflect on my life and the people that played a huge role in guiding me, I notice that I drew value out of those individuals and implemented their qualities into my characteristics. I saw the good in them and wanted to be like that. The same could be said when I looked up to the wrong type of people as a young man. They made a difference in my life as well. The self-damaging kind of difference, unfortunately. Now that I am an adult and in a fortunate position, I see how much of a massive impact I can make on others' lives. Being a positive influence on others is one of the best feelings you can have, especially after knowing what a bad influence can do to one's life. Understanding the power of persuasion is crucial to growth and establishing great relationships. Once you recognize this, you can decide the type of influence you want to be on others and who you would like to influence. People will never forget the interaction that they had with you. So why not make sure it's a memorable one that potentially makes a difference in them?

Your spouse, your work colleagues, your children, your boss, your family, etc., are all people that are in proximity of you, being able to impact their lives positively. Ask yourself, how would I like to be remembered? Do I want to impact, provoke some thoughts, or enlighten others? Do I want my experience with others to be long-lasting and meaningful?

I was at a 10X Growth Conference in Miami and listened to a well know American Bishop give me some great advice. He said (paraphrasing) "that your next opportunity is in the words you speak." So many people don't realize their ability to impact others and miss their chance to let their words resonate with others. When you interact with someone, that is your opportunity to make a real connection and positively influence their lives. Even if you don't stay in contact with them, they will never forget the conversation and feeling they had when they spoke with you. Think of someone that you admire and highly respect in your life.

It could be a family member, friend, or teacher. There was something that they probably said that you have and always will remember. That's the power of words. That's the opportunity that the Bishop was talking about. Their moment with you was to impact and have their words stick with you. People will forever remember anything profound that you say if it moves them. This is an example of why you should think about how and why you should get clear on the words you speak and the impact you want to make on someone when you have a conversation with them. One simple positive interaction can change someone's life forever.

HAVING THE RIGHT INFORMATION

Having the right information is crucial for various reasons and is often better than having none. Making decisions while having the wrong information can be devastating because it will cause you to waste time and energy on things you could've avoided. Time spent on the wrong people, business ventures, and faulty decision-making only follows destruction. Having a mentor will help you eliminate some of this wasted time. You can cut out years of unnecessary mistakes if you have a good mentor.

A good mentor will let you know all the mistakes they've made, how they would've avoided them, and what the best course of action should be for you. Then, the mentor will guide you on what will be best for you at your particular point in life. The ability to shave off years of wasted time and energy is valuable because you can accomplish your goals faster. The correct information will put you on the path to success and align you with the best decisions to help you fulfill your purpose in life.

Our time is precious, and a good mentor knows that. Therefore, they understand that you need information that will bypass as many potential mistakes as possible. Of course, you can't avoid some things, but wouldn't it be nice to prevent the majority of them or at least know what to expect? Think back on the mistakes that you may have made in the past that were devastating to you. There are some things that you wish you would've been able to avoid entirely, right? But, with the right mentor, you can because they have done it and figured out what they should've done. They've made mistakes and are letting you use their life as an example. After looking back at my life and noticing that I made terrible choices, I wanted to be in a mentorship position. I wanted to be a role model for people who felt lost, people who are not living their potential, and those who are craving that positive direction from someone who has made good and the best life decisions.

STAGES THAT PEOPLE NEED MENTORSHIP THE MOST

When I think about *when* people need mentorship the most in their lives, there are a couple of different times that I believe are important for people to receive this. The most obvious time would be when they are children. Children are very vulnerable and need it the most. In addition, the type of things that children learn when they are young will last forever. So, it is the best time to be a great mentor to them.

Parents should consider themselves a mentor first and a parent second. Children who lack guidance from their parents often grow up seeking mentorship. Direction is what children crave the most. I think it's the most critical time to make a substantial positive impact on their lives. This is the foundation of their thought process for the rest of their lives. They will build off this mindset, and if they have someone who is a robust role model in their life, they will retain this guidance forever. They may deviate from the advice here and there in their lifetime, but they never forget the intent and conversations they had with the people who cared about them the most and who they can tell have their best interest in mind.

It is much easier for a child to learn valuable information the first time rather than have to relearn it as an adult. Believe me. I had to rewire my entire thought process to get the correct information as an adult. The things that my mentor taught me were very new to me. I had never heard anyone speak about potential, massive action, and purpose. Once his (Cardone) mindset was introduced, he provoked some very intriguing thoughts that I wanted to continue to explore deeply. I got obsessed with understanding this way of thinking and immediately knew I needed to restructure my thinking to be like this individual. When you find the right mentor, you know that the words they speak are for you, and there's an undeniable attraction to this new mindset you have been introduced to.

That is how you know you have found the right mentor. It's imperative to acknowledge that feeling and to keep learning from this person more and more. Soon enough, you will notice your mindset shift and look at things from a new perspective. New relationships and conversations will develop, and new opportunities will appear. Your life will start to change in a very positive and meaningful way. This is a beautiful thing and most likely is what your life lacked.

If you feel you are missing something in your life, you are. That's when you know you need to seek something new. So, pay attention to those thoughts that you are having and never ignore that feeling of something more that you crave.

We are all meant for something more in our lives, and a lot of times, all we need is that mentor to come along and introduce us to new possibilities and help us tap into our full potential. Mentors create new ideas to reflect upon and show us how to manifest and execute them. Mentors help us envision and accomplish our long-term goals. Usually, at this point in our lives, we are entering our adult life and craving insight into our highest self-worth. That is why children and early adulthood are the two most important times mentorship is needed.

BE THAT MENTOR IN YOUR FAMILY

I don't come from a line of entrepreneurs in my family. I had to *be* the change. I chose to be an example for everyone that is in my life. I had to rewire my thinking in my thirties as an adult. It was not easy, and it took a lot of hard work. I have accomplished many things in the last seven years of my life that my friends and family have admired. They have seen my adversities because many went through them with me. I believe that there is a mentor in every family.

The question is, do they have the right or wrong information? Identifying misinformation is vital because you can spend years thinking that you are doing the right things based on what you learned from someone you admire. I challenge you to be that person in your family who separates yourself from the average thinker.

Set the tempo, be extraordinary, and push others in your family to improve and succeed. Be the *go-to* source for positive guidance and beneficial thinking. Thinking that will transform lives. Your family is in your immediate proximity for you to provide this guidance. If you have done great things and impacted others, you should be available to be that person for those who have watched you achieve this greatness.

HOW A MENTOR AND MENTEE WILL BENEFIT YOU

Having a mentor and being a mentee is a powerful experience! The process will uplift, challenge, and build confidence in both persons by accomplishing goals, hitting targets, increasing potential, overcoming adversity, crossing bridges, and pushing through obstacles that will strengthen you. The challenges you conquer together will be rewarding. While a mentee loves to grow and improve, a mentor loves to make a positive impact and help their mentee substantially develop.

Confidence results from going through the journey together, completing tasks, creating new opportunities, and increasing your potential. The momentum keeps driving that purpose to help others and help yourself. It becomes attractive and addicting. Everyone loves to be better at things. But unfortunately, most people get comfortable and go through life without getting the proper guidance on improving and getting information on how to get to the next level.

A mentor's goal is to show you how to break out of everyday behaviors and make significant changes. To replace bad habits with great ones and to identify valuable relationships from toxic ones. A mentor should show you how to get into suitable rooms with influential atmospheres. To be the best version of yourself that you can be and one of the most beneficial things a mentor can do for you is teach you how to invest in yourself.

FINDING YOUR PURPOSE

A good mentor will help you find your purpose in life and business; if you don't know your why, you may be aimless in your actions. Or even worse, doing things for writing reasons. I didn't find my purpose until I was thirty-eight years old. I thought I knew what I wanted. I did some things for the wrong reasons at times in my life. I can tell you from personal experience that things became so much easier for me when I found my purpose. My vision became clear, my actions aligned with my goals, and I always contributed to my purpose.

One of the most valuable things my mentor taught me was to write down my goals. This single habit has been essential to my life but takes discipline and routine. However, it is one of the best habits that you can ever implement in your life. Once I started to do this, it was a game changer for me. My mentor says that if something is worth doing once in your life, why only do it once?

Most of us write our goals down once a year when that magical New Year's Day comes around. What usually happens is that we forget what we wrote down or don't take it earnestly. I once heard a good friend say that the brain does this strange thing where it takes the things you write down seriously. Your brain will say to itself that if you're writing it down, then it must be important. Therefore, you are more likely to remember the importance of it. As a result, you are forty-eight percent more likely to achieve your goals when you write them down.

Most people never seek out their purpose or ignore the thought. We all had that moment where we asked ourselves, what am I meant to do with my life? I had that thought several times. This is normal and indicates that you are an ambitious person who just needs the right mentor. Unfortunately, most people go about life, as usual, without taking action on this pursuit they know is necessary. You can waste so much of your life and feel unfulfilled by never finding your purpose. When I found mine, it was a beautiful feeling of certainty, and I instantly knew that my life would change.

I began to make sure that every decision I made would benefit my purpose and contribute to my goals in life: short-term and long-term. When I established my purpose, it provided a real sense of direction for me. You will know when you're sure about your purpose because the feeling is undeniable and intense.

If you have not yet found your purpose in life, this should be one of the first things you discuss with your mentor. I think it is essential because it will drive all of the decisions that you make. It will provide you with clarity. It will give you confidence and make you feel outstanding about yourself. It may not be an immediate thing that you can establish, but you need to put a lot of thought into it because it is necessary to achieve your goals and be fulfilled. You should think about it daily and make it a part of your life. This is your primary focus and will dictate how you operate your life. We all have and need a purpose to drive us. So, when that question comes up in your head, don't ignore it. Embrace it. Put thought into it until it is established.

HOW TO FIND THE RIGHT MENTOR FOR YOU

These days you can find an abundance of inspirational people who do various things as mentors. With social media, getting your message out to the world and attracting people into your ecosystem is much easier. Mentors on social media understand the power of this and exploit it very much. So how do you find the right mentor for you? First, you want to ensure that the person you ultimately put your trust in has your best interest and is not doing it for money and publicity.

There are many people on this planet, and you will never agree with one person one hundred percent. Look for someone who you agree most and often with. The ideal approach would be to observe and study the individuals you consider taking advice from closely. After getting a handful of prospects, see who you agree with the most. They likely have a book they wrote or content they post regularly. Take a close look at these to see if anything they have done or spoken about resonates with you deeply. This will indicate if this person is speaking to you and could be the right mentor for you.

When considering a mentor, I followed and took advice from too many people. I realized some of the information I would hear from one person would contradict or be unaligned with the other person I was taking advice from. That's when I realized that it made sense to commit and focus on one person to learn from; someone aligned with my values, morals, and impact. It's crucial to find your mentor's *why* in their mission.

When I first read my mentor's book, it tremendously impacted me to the point where I knew his reason for wanting to help others, and I felt a connection. I was attracted to his purpose. It inspired me to make some immediate changes in my life. That is the power of one's message. We all have this same power.

THE POWER OF A GREAT MESSAGE

The power of your why. The power of influence. We all can impact other people's lives. You are and have already been doing this since you were born. You've changed your parents and family's lives as a baby and a sibling. At school, you've changed your friend's and teachers' lives. Would you rather be a person who unknowingly impacts others? Or would you like to solidify specific messages to these people and have them so inspired that they let you know exactly how you've helped them and what it means to them?

Everybody, including yourself, has a story and your message attracts people. When I realized the power of my story, I intertwined it with my message and confidently told it to others so they would put their trust in me to help them. Words are currency. Words are powerful. The words that come out of your mouth can determine the type of people you attract. Words determine the actions you take, along with your mindset. A mentor recognizes the power in their words and is aware of their impact.

THE POWER OF PEOPLE

Mentors have built powerful relationships. They also have great resources you can usually tap into for information or value. This allows you to increase your connections and networking web. As a result of doing this, you are now working on the most valuable currency, collaboration.

People need people. We need each other to create opportunities in our lives. My mentor once told me, "There has never been something great that just one person built." He was right. You must establish new relationships and continuously put yourself in positions to meet new people.

Other people have the resources, information, and guidance that we need. You could be one relationship away from getting that new job, a new big deal, or one connection away from meeting someone that will change your life forever. That's why it's important to keep getting to know people who want to see you succeed in life and business.

The relationships you form can end up being more in the future. You never know when you may need a great person to help you. You never know when you can be a big help to someone. So, keep good people in your corner and stay in good people's corners.

UNCONSCIOUS MENTORING

Did you know you've been mentored your entire life? Every day by the world around you and the garbage society throws at you. The poor advice you received from people in your life along the way. This is why actively seeking great information to help you accomplish your goals will significantly guide you. Without being mentored, you subconsciously take advice and collect data from anyone, social media, family members, coworkers, teammates, and even spouses. These are sources that are consistently coming at you with floods of information.

You need to decide what type of contagiousness you want in your life and make a choice to actively put yourself in those environments while being able to block out the information that is not helpful to you and your life. Keep in mind someone is always looking up to you. So even though society has taught you to lay low, don't get too much attention; someone somewhere is watching and learning from you.

MISGUIDED EDUCATION

Mentors who show you how to establish financial freedom are one of the essential benefits to a mentee. Unfortunately, because most people don't have the proper guidance regarding money, they are taught to save pennies and value money rather than use it as a resource and tool. Unsurprisingly, the educational system is flawed and not designed to teach or promote entrepreneurship or show you the proper ways to handle money. In my opinion, the educational system is designed to teach people how to be complacent, get a job that pays well, and have a good retirement plan. It is not structured to show you how to create your income.

This is why most people grow up with the wrong information about money and never learn how to generate, invest, and increase it. A good mentor will stress the importance of money and show you how to do this. Unfortunately, this is a topic that most people have to reprogram themselves with because they have been incorrectly conditioned for so long by the school system.

There are several ways to generate and multiply income that people are unaware and scared of simply because they have the wrong information about it. Therefore, it's necessary to make sure that you find a mentor with a genuine interest in getting you the correct information when it comes to money. In addition, make sure that you find a mentor that has your best interest in your financial freedom.

BE THE COACH

Having control of your life is vital to the level of success that you achieve. Once I started to take accountability for the outcome of my life, things changed. Once I began to re-evaluate my commitment level regularly, things changed. Several people were looking up to me, making me more aware of who I was influencing. The first thing that needed to happen was for me to be the mentor and coach of my own life before anything. The more I hold myself accountable, the more I can ensure others are doing the same thing to become better.

Being the mentor to others that I needed growing up is a big reward. Often, the person looking for mentorship might just need someone to hold them responsible, which is key to a successful mentorship. Once they have someone that will keep their hand, an action plan can be put in place so that the steps needed to accomplish the goals are being performed. Be direct and assertive as a mentor. Your respect will be earned when you operate this way.

IMPORTANCE OF ACCOUNTABILITY IN MENTORSHIP

You may have noticed that I have referenced the word "accountability" several times in the last few chapters. That is because accountability is the missing ingredient in most people's lives. A good portion of the population just wanders through life without taking the value and importance of accountability seriously. Yet, it is one of the essential traits one can have established in life.

Most people do not like to take accountability, therefore, place control in the hands of others by simply defaulting to not taking ownership of any outcome. They are quick to point the finger or step aside so they don't look bad or put themselves in a situation that may require them to take action.

Accountability requires immediate action and usually involves problem-solving, taking ownership of mistakes, and putting yourself on the front line. Unfortunately, these are situations that the average person does not like because society has taught us to fly under the radar and not put ourselves in the crosshairs of embarrassment, loss, or vulnerability.

When you choose to be accountable, you face the path of resistance. These moments make you stronger as a person. It builds your confidence because you choose to face more adversity and consistently overcome it. You become more credible when you become someone with a significant amount of accountability. You gain more respect because you are doing what most people are not.

You'll begin to feel empowered that you are taking control of your life in a major way. This results in admiration from others. I had clients hire me for this exact reason alone. On the other hand, a good mentor will also be open to being held accountable and receiving constructive criticism so that they can be better and improve on their effectiveness.

GETTING IN THE RIGHT ROOMS

One of the things that I learned by surrounding myself with entrepreneurs, business owners, and high-performance individuals is that you need to continuously put yourself in rooms with people who are more successful than you. People who have valuable information. People who have done massive things in their life and have achieved incredible things through their actions. I used to think the best room to be in was where everyone pats you on the back, strokes your image, and praises you for all your accomplishments.

However, I soon realized that there was no growth in those rooms. There is no challenge. There is no motivation to be better and better each day. The individuals at the top of their game who have done something of substantial worth are the ones you want to be around if you genuinely want to commit to greatness, manifest your purpose, and elevate your potential. Although showing up is the best first step that you can take and is the first rule of success, you should go to these events or gatherings to extract valuable information from these folks.

The other intention should be to exchange contact information with these people. Exchanging information, wisdom, and guidance from others who have done less than you or perhaps less ambitious than you are not the ones you should be surrounding yourself with too often. Networking is one of the most extraordinary actions you can take to build yourself up. You are one person away from your next ample opportunity.

I've had so many great connections, and doors opened for me due to showing up to these events and surrounding myself with people who are more successful than me. It has changed my life, and as I continue to climb and be a better businessman, father, and partner, I still get into rooms with the connections and information I need from the best types of people.

MENTORSHIP DURING DISCOURAGEMENT

A great mentor will influence you in positive ways. When you start to live your life differently and make big changes to improve your mindset and status, you will lose friends and family members and attract haters. Mentors know this all too well. This will especially happen more and more during your elevation. People will start to distance themselves from you. They will tell you that you have changed, not in a good way. They will assume that you may think that you are too good for them.

This is an unfortunate part of being appropriately mentored, but necessary. It happens because you are now separating yourself from ordinary and average thinkers. Don't be surprised when you get this response from some of your family, friends, and even your spouse. It's the best time to see who is in your corner and there to support you through this pivotal time. Having a mentor will help you stay on track when the haters, discouragement, and distractions come. Doubts and setbacks are certain.

When you have a solid mentor in your life, they help to get you back into better spirits during these times, and you should lean on them. They are interested in ensuring that you stay mentally healthy and will show you practical ways to keep yourself in that positive head space.

EPILOGUE

This book was written to give you an overview of the importance of mentorship and to understand the different perspectives it plays in life and what to look for as a mentor and a mentee. The purpose was to understand these various factors so you can have the best experience in a mentorship or mentee setting. My goal was to bring awareness that you are, have been, and will be a mentor at some point in your life. Use my experiences as an example of what and what not to do when it comes to mentorship. No matter your life age, you can find value in this book. It's intended to provoke valuable thoughts about mentorship and having the right information. Use this tool to find the best mentor for you and ensure that you are the best mentor to others who look up to you.

ABOUT BEN

Ben focuses on mentoring individuals and business owners to commit to greatness, manifest their purpose, and elevate to their potential. He has dedicated himself to influencing a positive mindset in entrepreneurs and those with high ambitions to generate massive results in their lives and businesses.

With his wide variety of life experiences, he has seen what works and doesn't work well for most people.

He was raised in a city with one of the nation's highest crime rates. He was misguided for 35 years before becoming a multi-success business owner, author, public speaker, and business partner with Grant Cardone and Lightspeed Virtual Training.

He has faced numerous adversities and knows what it takes to overcome these challenges that most of us go through. He teaches several strategies to become successful and enlightens people of all ages on the various aspects of mentorship.

His message is clear……..

Find A Mentor. Be The Mentor.